Funnier Bone Jokes

Brainless Birthday JOKES to Tickle Your FUNNY BONE

Felicia Lowenstein Niven

Enslow Elementary
an imprint of
Enslow Publishers, Inc.
40 Industrial Road
Box 398
Berkeley Heights, NJ 07922
USA
http://www.enslow.com

Enslow Elementary, an imprint of Enslow Publishers, Inc.

Enslow Elementary® is a registered trademark of Enslow Publishers, Inc.

Library of Congress Cataloging-in-Publication Data

Niven, Felicia Lowenstein.

Brainless birthday jokes to tickle your funny bone / by Felicia Lowenstein Niven.

p. cm. — (Funnier bone jokes)

Includes index.

Summary: "Read jokes, limericks, tongue twisters, and knock-knock jokes about birthdays. Also find out fun facts about this celebration"—Provided by publisher.

ISBN 978-0-7660-4121-9

1. Birthdays—Humor. 2. Wit and humor, Juvenile. I. Title.

PN6231.B47N58 2013

818'.60208—dc23

2012007700

Future editions

Paperback ISBN: 978-1-4644-0179-4 EPUB ISBN: 978-1-4645-1092-2

Single-User PDF ISBN: 978-1-4646-1092-9 Multi-User PDF ISBN: 978-0-7660-5720-3

Printed in the United States of America

082012 Lake Book Manufacturing, Inc., Melrose Park, IL

10 9 8 7 6 5 4 3 2 1

To Our Readers: We have done our best to make sure all Internet Addresses in this book were active and appropriate when we went to press. However, the author and the publisher have no control over and assume no liability for the material available on those Internet sites or on other Web sites they may link to. Any comments or suggestions can be sent by e-mail to comments@enslow.com or to the address on the back cover.

Every effort has been made to locate all copyright holders of material used in this book. If any errors or omissions have occurred, corrections will be made in future editions of this book.

Enslow Publishers, Inc., is committed to printing our books on recycled paper. The paper in every book contains 10% to 30% post-consumer waste (PCW). The cover board on the outside of each book contains 100% PCW. Our goal is to do our part to help young people and the environment too!

Illustration Credits: © clipart.com, pp. 4 (top), 13 (top), 14 (top), 25, 29 (bottom), 33 (left), 38 (bottom) 40 (bottom); Gerald Kelley, pp. 33 (right), 36; Photos.com: Bob Ash, p. 43 (bottom), Charles_Richard, p. 31 (bottom), Dynamic Graphics, pp. 6 (bottom), 12, 20, Frazer Worth, p. 11 (top), James Horvath, p. 31 (top), Roman Dekan, p. 8 (top), Toby Bridson, p. 30 (top), v0lha, p. 18 (top), Waldemar Neumann, p. 18 (bottom); Shutterstock.com, pp. 1, 3, 4 (bottom), 5, 6 (top), 7, 8 (bottom), 9, 10, 11 (middle, bottom), 13 (middle, bottom), 14 (bottom), 15, 16, 17, 18 (middle), 19, 21, 22, 23, 24, 26, 27, 28, 29 (top), 30 (bottom), 32, 34, 35, 37, 38 (top), 39, 40 (top), 41, 42, 43 (top), 44.

Cover Illustration: Shutterstock.com (front and back cover)

The limericks on pages 4 and 39 are reprinted with permission from Margaret "Meps" Schulte. Tongue twisters on pages 33 and 34 courtesy of Calan Ree, GingerDead.com. Special thanks to Virgil Keys for the limerick on page 33.

Contents

1 Birthday Basics

What do you always get on your birthday?

Another year older!

Knock knock.

Who's there?

Abby.

Abby who?

Abby birthday!

What does every birthday end with?

The letter y!

What did the big candle say to the little candle?

"You're too young to go out."

What did the tape say to the birthday presents?

"Mind if I stick around?"

Limerick

There's a guy who I proudly call Dad,
And a mighty fine birthday he had.
To make such a great man, it
Takes years on this planet.
But I won't tell his age (he'd get mad).

DID YOU KNOW?

A joke is something that makes people laugh.

I wish to wish the wish you wish to wish.

What goes up but never comes down?

Your age.

A tongue twister is a group of words with similar sounds. But try to say them fast. It's very hard to do.

Why are birthdays good for you?

The more you have, the longer you live.

Why do we put candles on top of a birthday cake?

Because it's too hard to put them on the bottom!

DID YOU KNOW?

No birthday would be complete without singing "Happy Birthday to You." But did you know that the song was written by two sisters, Patty and Mildred Hill? It's true! The tune was first published in 1893 under the name "Good Morning to All." Years later, Patty changed the words to the familiar birthday song we know today. The entire song was published in 1935. Today, it is one of the three most popular songs in the English language.

Limerick

This party is going to be great;
Been waiting so long for this date.
Got ready and dressed,
So I'd look my best.
Now I've only four hours to wait!

Picky people package presents perfectly.

WHAT IS A LIMERICK?

A limerick is a funny poem that rhymes. Lines 1, 2, and 5 rhyme one way. Lines 3 and 4 rhyme another.

What grows down when it grows up?

A goose.

2 Wild About Animals

Knock knock.

Who's there?

Hippo.

Hippo who?

Hippo birthday to you, hippo birthday to you . . .

Where do you find a birthday present for a cat?

In a cat-alogue!

What does a clam do on his birthday?

He shell-abrates!

Limerick

A tiger escaped from the zoo.
With nothing especially to do—
Lured by the sound,
A party she found,
And caused an extreme ballyhoo.

What did the elephant wish for on his birthday?

A trunk full of gifts.

FUN FACT

Are you a rat or a rabbit? The Chinese calendar names each year after one of twelve animals. That means the year you were born could be a rat or a rabbit. It also could be an ox, tiger, dragon, snake, horse, monkey, sheep/goat, rooster, dog, or pig. Each animal comes with a certain personality. For example, rats are smart and charming. Dogs are patient and kind. What's your Chinese sign? Does it fit your personality?

Clumsy Kitty kindles candles clumsily.

What do you give a 900-pound gorilla for his birthday?

I don't know, but you better hope he likes it!

What does a cat like to eat on his birthday?

Mice cream and cake!

Knock knock.

Who's there?

Omar.

Omar who?

Omar goodness! Your present escaped!

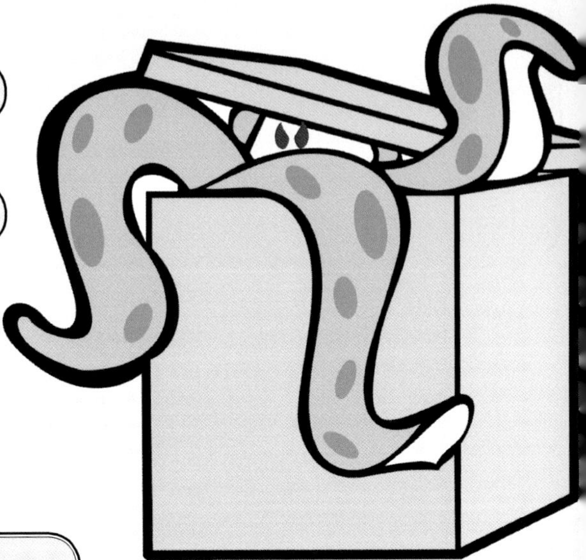

What has wings and a long tail, and wears a bow?

A birthday pheasant!

What kind of party do horses have on their birthday?

A birth-hay party!

Limerick

There was a young sheep named Lu-lu,
Who was turning the ripe age of two.
She couldn't yet spell,
Which was just as well—
Her friends wrote,
Happy Birthday to Ewe!

Tattletale turtle turns twenty-two today.

What party game do rabbits like to play?

Musical hares.

Limerick

Two silly rabbits couldn't agree
On a gift for their friend chimpanzee.
"Let's not get him any;
And save a pretty penny."
"That's bananas," his friend said with glee.

3 Just for Boys

What did the birthday balloon say to the pin?

"Hi, Buster."

Were any famous men born on your birthday?

No, just little babies.

Why couldn't prehistoric man send birthday cards?

The stamps kept falling off the rocks.

DID YOU KNOW?

In the early 1800s, children's birthday parties were times to teach manners.

What was the average age of a caveman?

Stone Age.

What did the birthday hat say to the scarf?

"You hang around while I go on ahead."

Hard-hearted Hank hankers for happy birthday harmonies.

FUN FACT

Long ago, people thought evil spirits would be attracted to a person on his or her birthday. Family and friends surrounded the person to keep away harm. They even brought gifts for the birthday person, and noisemakers to scare off the spirits. That was the start of the first birthday parties!

How does an ogre count to fifteen years old?

On his fingers!

Limerick

There once was a
household of boys,
Whose mode was
continuous noise.
But when birthdays
were here,
Good manners
appeared—
They were hoping for
piles of new toys.

Limerick

There once was a young boy named Jack
Who was hungry for some sort of snack.
Birthday cake he did spy,
And quick as a sigh,
He stuffed it right into his sack.

The birthday boy brought a brass banjo.

Knock, knock.

Who's there?

Gus.

Gus who?

Gus how old I am today!

Knock, knock!

Who's there?

Freddy.

Freddy who?

Freddy to open your presents?

4 Just for Girls

Did you hear about the dancer's birthday?

It was a tappy one!

How many presents can you put in an empty box?

One. After that, it's not empty.

Which burns longer, a blue birthday candle or a pink one?

Neither. They both burn shorter.

Knock, knock!

Who's there?

Dewey.

Dewey who?

Dewey have to keep saying these jokes?

Knock, knock.

Who's there?

Botany.

Botany who?

Botany good presents lately?

DID YOU KNOW?

The color pink is usually associated with girls. But over 100 years ago, baby boys were dressed in pink, too. It didn't become a "girl" color until about 1940.

Did you hear about the tree's birthday?

It was a sappy one!

How do we know Rapunzel used to have fun at birthday parties?

She liked to let her hair down.

What did Cinderella say when her birthday party photographs weren't ready?

"Some day my prints will come."

There was a young princess named Jean
Who was going to turn seventeen.
For her birthday feast,
Seventeen cakes at least:
"I like choices, know what I mean?"

Limerick

**You're ten and you want a cell phone
So that you can be on your own.
Your birthday surprise
Makes you think twice—
A phone that will only call home!**

FUN FACT

Each day, there are at least 15 million people in the world celebrating a birthday. Do you know any of them?

Patsy picks pretty papered packages.

Limerick

There once was a young girl named Pam,
Who got in a bit of a jam.
Just one small mishap—
The cake fell in her lap—
Said she, "Well, now I don't look very glam."

5 Double Whammy:

Holiday Birthdays

What's an elf's favorite kind of birthday cake?

Shortcake!

What did the reindeer sing to Father Christmas on his birthday?

"Freeze a jolly good fellow!"

Where does a snowman put his birthday candles?

On his birthday flake!

DID YOU KNOW?

Christians celebrate the birth of Jesus of Nazareth on December 25, Christmas. But historians believe that Jesus was probably born in the spring.

What do you wear to a Thanksgiving birthday dinner?

A har-vest!

What do George Washington, Abraham Lincoln, and Martin Luther King Jr. all have in common?

They were all born on holidays!

What would you get if you crossed a Patriot with a birthday cake?

Yankee Strudel!

Knock, knock.

Who's there?

Justin.

Justin who?

Justin time for the party!

Santa's seven sleighs slid sideways.

Limerick

The presents lie under the tree.
There's some for you and some for me.
But for lucky Fred
He's got double instead;
Those Christmas birthdays are very lucky!

Limerick

You may think it's Christmas, but wait,
There's another event on this date.
It's the day of my birth,
A great occasion on Earth
So don't think your presents can be late.

FUN FACT

Many famous people were born on holidays. Juliette Gordon Low, founder of the Girl Scouts, was born on Halloween. Sir Isaac Newton, the scientist who discovered gravity, was born on Christmas Day. Betsy Ross was born on New Year's Day. Advice columnist twins Abigail Van Buren (Dear Abby) and Ann Landers were born on the Fourth of July.

Knock, knock.

Who's there?

Wendy.

Wendy who?

Wendy party ends, can I play with your presents?

If two witches would watch two watches, which witch would watch which watch?

6 Special Birthdays

Why was the broom late to Carlita's Quinceañera?

It overswept.

What is the best thing to put into a Quinceañera cake?

Your teeth.

DID YOU KNOW?

A Quinceañera is a celebration of a girl's fifteenth birthday in many Latin American countries. In some ways it is like a Sweet Sixteen. A bar or bat mitzvah is a birthday ceremony for Jewish boys (bar) or girls (bat). Both occasions celebrate a child growing into an adult.

What did the pin say to the corsage?

Move over, bud!

What is black and white and red all over?

A tuxedoed bar mitzvah boy who just got kissed by Aunt Leah!

Many memorable mitzvah moments made Moishe's bar mitzvah momentous.

What do you get when you cross candy with sweat socks?

A Sweat Soxteen!

Stunningly stylish stupendous Sweet Sixteen success!

FUN FACT

It used to be that at age sixteen, a girl was considered old enough to be married. Today, Sweet Sixteen parties celebrate girls' becoming young women. The parties can be very fancy. Actress and singer Miley Cyrus spent her Sweet Sixteen in a private party with 5,000 fans at Disneyland.

Limerick

When they raised her up on the chair,
Her view of her guests couldn't compare.
High above the crowd,
She said, much too loud,
Look at all of those men without hair!

Knock, knock.

Who's there?

Sew.

Sew who?

Sew many presents, so little time.

Limerick

Happy birthday from Mom and Dad!
It's not in a box—don't be mad.
Instead it's a car!
Keys? Gas? There you are!
Is this the best present you've had?

Knock knock.

Who's there?

Wanda.

Wanda who?

Wanda wish you a happy bar mitzvah!

7 Birthdays Around the World

What travels around the world but stays in one corner?

A stamp!

Which people traveled the most for their birthdays?

The Romans.

Belgians bake bodacious birthday cakes.

DID YOU KNOW?

What is Mom serving for your birthday? In China, it would be noodles, said to give the birthday child a long life. In Guyana, it would be chicken, duck, or lamb curry. Russian kids get birthday pies instead of cakes, with a message carved into the crust.

What's the greatest birthday present?

Hard to say, but it would take a lot to beat an African drum!

Did you hear about the French flag's birthday?

Oo-la-la . . . it was a flappy one!

Limerick

In Mexico, birthdays are neat;
Break the piñata for a sweet treat.
In the race for the candy,
The kids are so handy,
The adults—they just cannot compete!

Knock, knock.

Who's there?

Major.

Major who?

Major think about
your next birthday,
didn't I?

Limerick

In England, it's common to bake
Coins or rings in your birthday cake.
Coins mean you'll be rich;
Rings mean you'll get hitched.
One forkful determines your fate.

Knock, knock.

Who's there?

Irish.

Irish who?

Irish you a
happy birthday!

FUN FACT

Watch your bottom! In Ireland, children are given "birthday bumps." They are lifted by hands and feet and "bumped" on the floor—one bump for each year, plus one for good luck.

Pass the pole—pound the party piñata!

Greek grapes go great on birthday cakes.

8 Birthdays Gone Wrong

What usually comes after the monster lights his birthday candles?

The fire department!

Knock, knock.

Who's there?

Philip.

Philip who?

Philip on cake and you might skip dinner!

What candy is never on time?

Choco-late!

What five-letter word is spelled wrong by over 99 percent of college graduates?

The word wrong.

DID YOU KNOW?

Hold on to your ears! In Europe, people might pull them during your birthday celebration.

What is a tornado's favorite party game?

Twister!

Pointed party hats are perfect for puncturing people.

How can you tell you're getting old?

You go to an antique auction and three people bid on you!

Limerick

This year I have something to boast:
I remembered your birthday (almost).
This card may be late
but it's close to the date.
Let's pretend it got lost in the post.

Sign in school cafeteria: Shoes are required to eat cake in the cafeteria.

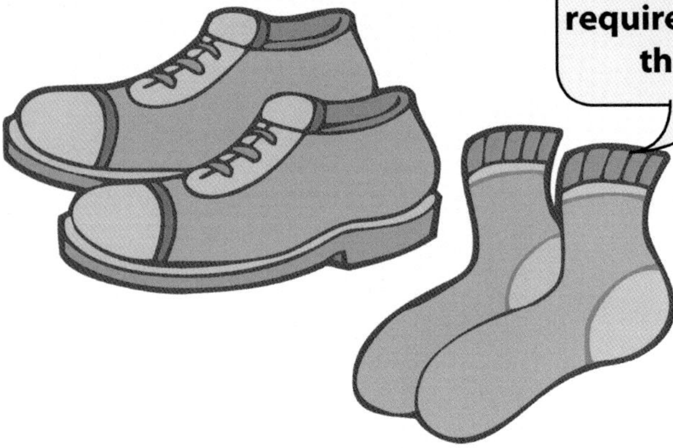

A student then wrote below: Socks can eat cake wherever they want.

Please provide presents or prepare to perish.

Limerick

The mom of a monkey named Drake
Had a banana cake to make.
She found the design
And thought it'd be fine,
But the oven just wouldn't bake.

FUN FACT

Did you know? The song "Happy Birthday" was the first song performed in outer space. It's true! The *Apollo IX* astronauts sang it on March 8, 1969.

Giggling Gilda got a gaggle of gag gifts.

Knock, knock.

Who's there?

Jimmy.

Jimmy who?

Jimmy some ice cream and cake! It's my birthday!

Limerick

So your birthday is coming along,
With candles and wishes and song.
If, to blow out the fire,
Some help you require,
Perhaps you have lived much too long.

9 Recipe for Birthday Fun

What do they serve at birthday parties in heaven?

Angel food cake!

Why did the birthday cake go to the doctor?

He was feeling crumby.

Why was the birthday cake as hard as a rock?

Because it was marble cake!

DID YOU KNOW?

Early birthday cakes were more like bread. In Roman times, they were made of cereal grain mixed with water or wine and maybe yeast.

What did the ice cream say to the unhappy cake?

"Hey, what's eating you?"

Knock, knock.

Who's there?

Bacon.

Bacon who?

Bacon a cake for your birthday!

Which is the left side of a birthday cake?

The side no one ate yet.

A bit of better butter makes better birthday batter.

Knock, knock.

Who's there?

Ivan.

Ivan who?

Ivan a piece of
your cake!

Calvin ate a colossal collection of candy and cake.

Limerick

Happily, the little girls played,
Making birthday mud cakes in the glade.
Flowers, stones, and such
Were the final touch,
Once they iced the cakes with a spade.

FUN FACT

The world's largest birthday cake weighed 130,000 pounds. It was covered with nearly 40,000 pounds of icing. The cake was made in 2005 for the 100th birthday of Las Vegas, Nevada. Ingredients were donated by Sara Lee Foods. Party guests got to take away pieces that were as big as they could carry.

Limerick

There once was a lady named Kate,
Whose birthday was on this fine date.
She wanted a cake,
But her friends could not bake,
So her candles just sat on a plate.

10 Let's Party!

Why didn't the teddy bear want any more cake?

Because he was stuffed!

Bald Billy balanced birthday boxes beneath the banister.

Where do you hold a birthday party in California?

San Fran-Disco!

Where did the spaghetti go to dance on her birthday?

The meat ball!

DID YOU KNOW?

The most common American birthday is October 5. An average of 12,576 babies are born each year on this date. May 22 is the least common American birthday, with an average of 10,259 babies born on that date yearly.

Knock, knock.

Who's there?

Lena.

Lena who?

Lena little closer and I'll tell you what I got.

How did Darth Vader know what Luke Skywalker was getting for his birthday?

He felt his presents.

What did the girl name her birthday burger?

Patty!

Knock, knock.

Who's there?

Rabbit.

Rabbit who?

Rabbit up carefully; it's a present!

Games galore gave Glinda gobs of glee.

Limerick

A party's a time to have fun,
So we certainly hope you can come
And join in our mirth,
As we celebrate a birth,
And shake off the same old humdrum.

What did the lawyer name his daughter?

Sue.

When does a Friday birthday come before a Thursday birthday?
In the dictionary.

What did the oven say to the Little Leaguer's birthday cake?
Batter up!

FUN FACT

At first, only kings could have birthday celebrations. Maybe that's why the birthday boy or girl wears a crown? Cone-shaped hats are also popular at birthdays. They're fun, and worn by many different cultures.

Limerick

Pin the tail is a birthday game
Whose target can have different names:
Rabbit or donkey,
Bear, cat, or monkey,
It's all party fun just the same.

It's easy to make your own funny birthday card. Here's how to do it.

HERE'S WHAT YOU WILL NEED:

- A joke book
- A piece of construction paper
- Markers or crayons
- Other decorations, such as stickers, stamps, and pieces of wrapping paper (optional)

DIRECTIONS:

1. Choose one of the jokes or limericks in this book.
2. Fold the construction paper in half like a card.
3. Write the beginning of the joke or limerick on the front of the card.
4. Write the punch line on the inside of the card. If you use a limerick, write the last line on the inside of the card.
5. Use markers to illustrate the joke.
6. You can use other decorations, such as stickers, stamps, or even cutouts from wrapping paper, to make the card more special.
7. Remember to write on the back of the card, "Handmade by (your name)."
8. Finally, write your own special message to the birthday person—just as you would on a store-bought card.

Words to Know

ballyhoo—A noisy commotion.

bar mitzvah/bat mitzvah—A birthday ceremony for Jewish boys (bar) or girls (bat) to symbolize the change from childhood to adulthood.

glam—Glamorous, fancy, fascinating.

harmony—A pleasing song or tune in which several notes are played at the same time.

joke—Something said to make people laugh.

limerick—A funny five-line poem in which the first, second, and fifth lines rhyme, and the shorter third and fourth lines rhyme.

Quinceañera—A celebration of a girl's fifteenth birthday in many Latin American countries and cultures.

Sweet Sixteen—A celebration of a girl's sixteenth birthday in the United States.

tongue twister—A series of fun words with similar sounds that can be hard to say out loud.

Read More

Books

Dahl, Michael, Kathi Wagner, Aubrey Wagner, and Aileen Weintraub. *The Everything Kids' Giant Book of Jokes, Riddles & Brain Teasers.* Avon, MA: F + W Media, 2010.

Leno, Jay. *How to Be the Funniest Kid in the Whole World (or Just in Your Class).* New York: Aladdin Paperbacks, Simon & Schuster Children's Publishing, 2007.

Phillips, Bob. *Super Incredible Knock-Knock Jokes for Kids.* Eugene, OR: Harvest House Publishers, 2007.

Internet Addresses

Giggle Poetry
<http://www.gigglepoetry.com/>

Jokes & Humor—Yahoo! Kids
<http://kids.yahoo.com/jokes>

Jokes By Kids
<http://www.jokesbykids.com>

Index